Jesus,
You Did It Again!

Jesus, You Did It Again!

by
Reta Spears-Stewart
Illustrations by Phillip Secca
Edited by Hope Victoria

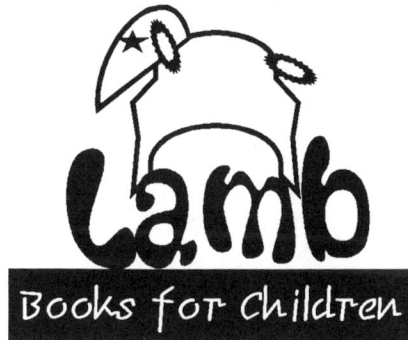

Books for Children

An imprint of

BARNABAS
Publishing Services
Springfield, Missouri U.S.A.

Jesus, You Did It Again!
Written by Reta Spears-Stewart
Illustrations by Phillip Secca
Edited by Hope Victoria
© 1991 by Reta Spears-Stewart
Second Edition, Published 1999
Lamb Books for Children
an imprint of
Barnabas Publishing Services
1845 S. Pickwick Ave.
Springfield, Missouri, 65804
U.S.A.

Library of Congress Catalog Card Number: 97-94838
ISBN 0-9638648-8-2

With very special thanks to
Rev. Dale O'Connell

Before there was anything anywhere,
    while Jesus was still living in Heaven...

He just said the Word...

...and everything happened everywhere.

Genesis 1:1,2,3

Once after Jesus came to earth, he and his mother, Mary, went to a wedding. In those days, it was important for wedding guests to have a special wine to bless the bride and groom. But that family ran out of wine for their friends.

7

Mary told the servants to do whatever Jesus said about the problem. Jesus told them to fill their water jars with plain old water. Then he just said the Word...

And when they tasted that water, it had become wedding wine. That was Jesus' first miracle. After that, many people believed in him. *John 2:3-10*

9

One day a soldier whose servant was dying came to see Jesus.

"Please, come quickly," said the soldier to Jesus, "and make my servant well."

But Jesus just said the Word...

...and the servant was well before the soldier got home!

Matthew 8:5-10

Once Jesus was teaching a whole hillside of people what God wants us to know. Then he noticed they were all getting hungry. So Jesus just said the Word...

...and one boy's lunch basket held a picnic for thousands of people!

John 6:8-12

Sometimes so many people came to see all the great things Jesus was doing, they couldn't all fit inside. Once the friends of a man who couldn't walk lowered him through a hole in the roof. Jesus just said the Word...

14

...and the man got up and carried his little mattress home with him.

Mark 2:2-5, 11

15

Another time, when Jesus was teaching outdoors, a man named Jairus begged Him to come and heal his little girl. Then someone told them the girl had already died. But Jesus went home with the man anyway. He just said the Word...

...and the little girl came back to life. *Mark 5:22, 35, 36, 41*

17

Once Jesus' friends were sailing on the sea when a super-
big windstorm came blowing along and scared them all silly.
Then they saw Jesus walking out to them on *top* of those waves

18

Jesus just said the Word...and his friends weren't afraid anymore.

John 6:16-21

One day, as Jesus and his friends were walking along, they saw a blind beggar. This time Jesus made some mud to put on the man's eyes.

Then he just said the Word...and the man could see.

John 9:1-7

Jesus' good friend Lazarus died. His sisters, Mary and Martha, told Jesus, "His body is in that cave." At first, Jesus felt sad and cried.

But then he just said the Word...and his friend Lazarus was alive again.

John 11:32-45

Jesus did a lot more miracles. He still does them today.
He just says the Word...

...and the sun rises, babies are born, birds sing, gardens grow, people get well, and friends love one another.

John 1:17